Bangkok travel guide book

Your Ultimate Travel Guide for Discovering the City's Attractions and Deep Cultural Insights.

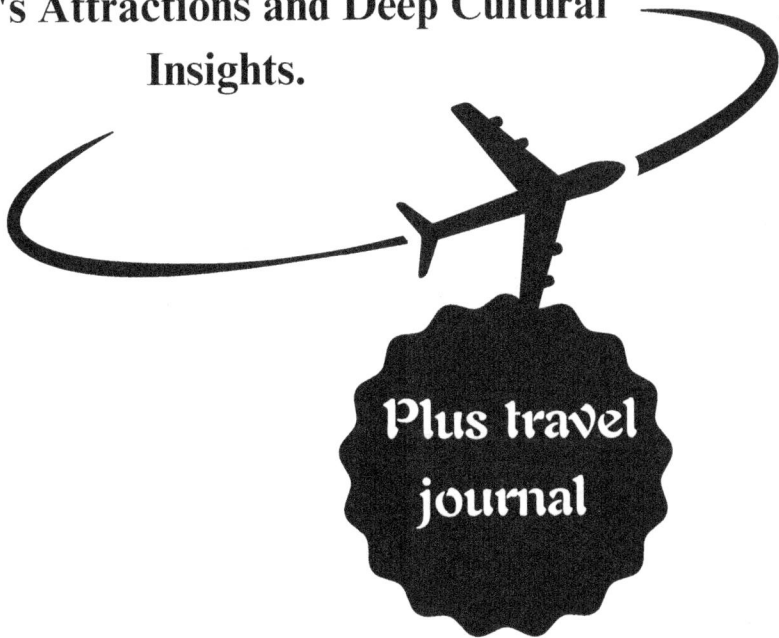

Plus travel journal

Javier L. Nixon

"Congratulations, intrepid reader! Unfurling the pages of this book was an absolutely splendid decision – get ready for a journey of literary delight!"

The information provided here is for general purposes only and should not be considered as professional advice. Users are encouraged to independently verify any information and exercise their own judgment when applying it. Use the information at your own discretion.

About Author

Javier L. Nixon is a seasoned author and avid tourist known for his vivid study of places worldwide. With a love for discovering the spirit of each place he sees, Nixon puts together rich storylines that go beyond standard travel books. His work shows a deep respect for cultural details and a dedication to giving readers with useful insights for a rewarding path. Having covered the world, Nixon's works often dig into the heart and soul of various places, catching their unique charm and character. His unique approach to trip writing blends entertaining stories with up-to-date knowledge, giving readers a complete and immersive experience. Nixon's commitment to sharing travel experiences stretches to his praised works, such as "Bangkok travel guide book" where he expertly takes readers through the charming streets of Bangkok, Thailand.

Through his books, Javier L. Nixon sparks wanderlust and urges travelers to accept the genuineness of each place, making him a go-to source for those wanting more than just a normal travel guide.

Table of contents

"Grab your literary snorkel and plunge headfirst into the ocean of words – it's a wild adventure waiting to unfold!"

Introduction to Bangkok

Welcome to the city of Angels

Bangkok is the capital and most important city in Thailand, with a population of over 10 million people. Thanks to its growing economic development and massive popularity as an international tourist destination, it has become one of Southeast Asia's most influential and modern cities.

Located on the banks of the country's main river, Chao Phraya, the city relied on a wide system of canals - khlong in Thai - for transport between the 16th and 19th centuries, leading to its nickname as the Venice of the East. On the subject of names, Bangkok's full Thai name has the Guinness World Record for "longest place name"! But at 168 letters of archaic language, most locals call it the much simpler Krung Thep, which translates roughly as "City of Angels".

Bangkok is Thailand's buzzing capital, home to the Grand Palace, countless historic temples, delicious cuisine that ranges from cheap eats to top-end gourmet experiences, and truly spectacular options for shoppers. It's no coincidence that Bangkok has become one of the world's great global cities. It only takes a day in the capital to understand why. Head to the islands in the south to indulge in a Thailand beach escape. The pristine beaches of Phuket, Samui, Krabi,Khao Lak, Phi Phi,and Chang are stunning and relaxing. These escapes are a great add-on to your Thailand or Asia itinerary and make for a fantastic winter or romantic getaway in their own right.

Bangkok is so full of life…everywhere. One cannot help but be caught up in the hustle and bustle, the crowds, congestion and food – all day and all night. This is not to be ignored but is to be experientially jumped into full throttle.

Thailand, country located in the centre of mainland Southeast Asia. Located wholly within the tropics, Thailand encompasses diverse ecosystems, including the hilly forested areas of the northern frontier, the fertile rice fields of the central plains, the broad plateau of the northeast, and the rugged coasts along the narrow southern peninsula.

Thailand, which has about the same land area as Spain or France, consists of two broad geographic areas: a larger main section in the north and a smaller peninsular extension in the south.

The main body of the country is surrounded by Myanmar (Burma) to the west, Laos to the north and east, Cambodia to the southeast, and the Gulf of Thailand to the south.

Peninsular Thailand stretches southward from the southwestern corner of the country along the eastern edge of the Malay Peninsula; Myanmar extends along the western portion of the peninsula as far as the Isthmus of Kra, after which Thailand occupies the entire peninsula until reaching its southern border with Malaysia at roughly latitude 6° N.

Brief History and Culture

Bangkok's culture is affected by the modern day, yet still keeps very proud links to its heritage and Buddhist faith. This culture can be found on every street corner, in the food, language, music, dance, the arts, and Buddhist shrines. "Bangkokians" are a warm and friendly people, giving with their welcoming smile, truly proud of their "Thai-ness", and usually too polite to show offence, anger or annoyance. Only a fool though, would dare mistake their kindness for weakness.

There are standards of manners that should be followed at all times in Bangkok, and Thailand more broadly. Thais take great joy in their government, especially the King. Visitors are well-advised to respect the awe in which Bangkokians hold the Thai Royal family.

Buddhism is the main faith in Bangkok, with monks, temples, spirit houses, Buddha pictures and statues everywhere you look. It is assumed that proper clothes be worn in churches, and shoes removed before entering. There is also a sizeable Muslim population spread around the city who are 100% Thai in every respect.

For Bangkokians, keeping a cool, peaceful and harmonious attitude at all times is important. Outward displays of bad anger, louder voice, threatening actions, fighting, or critical statements is generally avoided. Such behaviour serves no useful purpose in polite

Thai culture

The famous wai is used as a sign for both welcome and respect. A Wai needs the person to use both of his hands as if praying in front of his face. In general, it is thought to be a mark of respect to try to keep the head at a lower level than that of a senior or older person when talking to or passing them. Its not recommended for tourists to try to Wai others, as there is a complicated process involved. A smile or nod is enough to recognize a Wai given by hotel staff and so on.

On entering a private house, it is normal to always remove your shoes. The polite way to call an adult of similar, or older age is to use the term "Khun" before the person's first name.

Most Bangkokians are too polite to comment directly on behaviour that is rude, but you should be aware that their silence should not be confused for it is still hurtful.Looks and looks are important to Bangkokians.

Personal cleanliness is held in high regard by Thai people, when meeting them, dressed smartly, or at least properly, can be taken as the degree of respect you hold for them. Many homes and businesses have spirit houses on the land to allow the placement of gifts, flowers, foodstuffs such as sticky rice and rice whiskey. The goal of the Spirit House is to provide an attractive haven for the spirits, or celestial beings, who would otherwise live in the places filled by human houses, big trees, caves, hills, rivers etc. It is believed that the spirits are picky and mischievous, demanding respect from people and capable of doing great harm if they aren't given proper respect. This tradition perhaps helps put some light on the faith of Thai people in general.

During the rule of Rama I, Bangkok's beautiful Grand Palace and Wat Pho temple were built. His followers built yet more wats, or shrines, including Wat Arun as well as schools, museums and hospitals. Bangkok, .

and therefore Siam, like much of the rest of the world, was industrialising and modernising; with both government and building changes. Originally depending on canals as the main way to move through the city, by the late 19th century there were roads, bridges, the first trains, and even an electric tram service

While building was inspired by European styles, interestingly Bangkok, and Siam as a whole, were never invaded by the European forces. They were relatively safe due to their unified rule and as the rivalling French and British saw them as a peaceful bridge between Indochina (France) and India and Burma (Britain). Having said this, disagreements with the French did lead to Siam giving some land to the western power.

Essential Travel Tips

1.Get a good map

Bangkok can be confusing. The changing street names, the flowing river, the expressways to who-knows-where, the lack of clearly distinguishable areas. Sometimes it all seems like urban planning is seriously missing here. The solution? Arm yourself with a good map with street names in English and Thai. If Bangkok is a mean-spirited maze, consider this your loyal guide. Google Maps can be a big help, but you'd often need to further physically translate addresses that still show in Thai writing.

2.Beware of scammers

It starts with a nice stranger saying something along the lines of, "The Grand Palace is closed this afternoon". You thank them and tell them where you're from. Then, before you've even had a chance to shake their hands, you're holding the sides of a tuk-tuk as it whizzes towards sites your guidebook has never heard of – and pushy gem shops.

The general, but by no means universal, rule of thumb: a stranger who approaches you in the street isn't looking for a friendly chat.

3.Try a planned tour

A tour gets the parts that other ways of seeing Bangkok cannot. Yes, hitting the streets with just a trusty map in hand, does appeal to the daring in us. But ask yourself: are you here to enjoy Bangkok or what?

A walk is cheap and easily arranged (just book and show up). No practical problems, no getting lost, just a wonderful day out that takes back another exciting layer of The Big Mango.

4.Plan ahead

Bangkok is not an easily walkable city. Rather, making the most of this overwhelming sprawl of people, trade and culture takes a bit of planning… Work out what you want to see, where they are with a good offline or online map, then work out a sensible plan.

Taxis are likely to be necessary, as is a bit of dancing, but wherever possible use the favourites: the waterways, underground and Skytrain. Sight-wise, don't bite off more than you can chew – Bangkok's tastes are best savoured slowly.

5.Use the BTS and MRT regularly

Bangkok is famed for its smoke-belching tuk-tuks, hair-raising motorbikes, and exciting canal boats. But when it comes to getting around the city, the Skytrain and MRT are easily your most acceptable choices.

The Skytrain leaps above traffic, while the underground MRT whizzes, mole-like, beneath it. Both offer cool air-conditioning and are, in our opinion, the best products since the wheel, especially during hot Bangkok days. Get yourself a day or week pass and hop aboard.

6.Bangkok Taxi Tips

When taking a cab in Bangkok, follow these tips and your trip needn't be temper-fraying: avoid rush hour, insist your driver switch his meter on. If he refuses, get out and find another – they're usually plentiful.
Finally, make sure you leave nothing behind. There's nothing worse than watching your gaily-coloured cab whiz off into Bangkok's smoke, taking with it your belongings.

7.Carry a picture of your passport

Whether it's an unexpected demand from a local cop or a request from security at one of the city's swanky nightspots, having ID is a must in Thailand. The fact that you're 25 but look like you're hitting 40 doesn't really matter – showing who you are is a day-to-day detail, something the Thais are picky about. Instead of taking your passport around with you, and with it the constant fear of losing it, it's a good idea to bring a photocopy of it instead.

8.Carry a room card with Thai directions

Carrying a room card whenever you're out and about in Bangkok is an easy job. But this clever device, little more than a piece of paper with your hotel's address written on it in Thai, will save endless how-do-we-get-home problems.

Show it to your chosen driver and watch how his shrugs of total incomprehension quickly change to calming nods. Brilliant.

9.Dress properly for temple visit

Many of us want to get a bit of a tan when the sun is out, but it's important to remember that Buddhism is still a very central part of life in Thailand. So, when viewing temples, shoulders and anything above the knee should be covered up.

This is especially good advice for when visiting The Grand Palace, as you may be forced to rent a pair of loose pyjamas and a 1970s-style floral blanket if your clothing is deemed 'inappropriate'.

10. Thai National Anthem at 8am and 6pm

One of the most interesting sights for first-time guests to Bangkok happens every day at 8am and at 6pm. Both are when the Thai National Anthem is played in train stops, markets, and government buildings throughout the country.

Thai people will all stop what they are doing and stand quietly in respect, but will all continue with their busy lives on the beat of the last bell. As a stranger, it's polite to stop if you happen to hear this song being blared through a megaphone with thousands of people standing to attention.

Navigating Bangkok

Transportation Guide

Air fares to Thailand usually rely on the season, with the highest being approximately mid-November to mid-February, when the weather is best (with extra rates paid for trips between mid-Dec and New Year), and in July and August to coincide with school breaks. You will need to book several months in advance to get reasonably priced tickets during these busy times.

Planes

Return trips between the United States or Europe and Bangkok vary based on the place and the season, however they can be found for as little as US$ 400, and from the UK from £ 280 (US$ 355.50). As the saying goes, time is money, and straight flights or those with short stopovers are usually lot pricier than those with a long delay.

Travelling by plane from elsewhere in Asia can be very cheap too. It's usually under US$ 100 to fly from Vietnam, Cambodia and Singapore, for example; and often less than US$ 50 to journey to Bangkok from other places of Thailand, including the islands.

Most foreign planes land at Bangkok Suvarnabhumi Airport (BKK), which took over from Don Mueang Airport (DMK) as the city's main airport in 2006. The latter is largely used for local flights and some foreign flights from other places in Southeast Asia.

Bangkok Suvarnabhumi Airport

Since replacing DMK airport in 2006 as Bangkok's main airport, Suvarnabhumi is the place where most foreign guests fly into the Thai city. You've arrived - learn how best to get to the city after landing!

Suvarnabhumi International Airport (pronounced su-wan-na-poom) is one of the biggest international airports in Southeast Asia, the 21st busiest airport in the world, and the largest in the country. Opened in 2006, it acquired BKK as its code when the city's old main airport Don Mueang temporarily stopped business flights.

The airport is very modern and activities usually run smoothly. Its webpage has real-time information of entries and exits. Despite having just one terminal, it's huge (the world's fourth biggest single terminal building).

Getting to Bangkok from Suvarnabhumi

Airport taxi

Getting a cab is a simple, easy and quick way to reach the city centre. Depending on where exactly your accommodation is located, the journey will probably last around half an hour and the price on the meter will range from 250 THB (US$ 7.20) to 400 THB (US$ 11.50) plus the 50 THB (US$ 1.40) airport charge, paid directly to the driver, and toll charges of 25 THB (US$ 0.70) to 70 THB (US$ 2), which passengers also pay.

The cab stop is situated on floor 1, near the customs area. Follow the sign for Public Taxis and ignore touts offering "Official Taxis" in the airport, they'll overcharge! Make sure your driver agrees to use the meter.

Transfer help

Even easier and more comfortable is pre-booking a taxi service to pick you up from the airport and take you straight to your hotel. Your driver will wait for you in arrivals with your name on a sign, and you save time and effort trying to find a public car.

Airport Rail Link

The Airport Rail Link is a cheap and safe way to reach Bangkok city heart after getting at the airport. It connects the airport with the BTS (Skytrain) stop at Phaya Thai (45 THB (US$ 1.30), 30 minutes, from 6 am to midnight) and the MRT (Metro) stop at Phetchaburi (45 THB (US$ 1.30), 25 minutes, from 6 am to midnight).

From these places, you can reach your housing using Bangkok's public transport system, or hop in a cab or tuk-tuk in the city centre.

Local Buses

Travellers on a tight budget and those wanting the real local experience might want to hop on a local bus from the airport. If this choice is for you, hop on the free shuttle bus at Suvarnabhumi, which will take you to the public transport hub about 2 miles (3 km) away, from which the public buses leave. The most common buses for heading to the city centre are line 551 to BTS Victory Monument station (40 THB (US$ 1.10), frequent from 5 am to 10 pm) and 552 to BTS On Nut (20 THB (US$ 0.60), frequent from 5 am to 10 pm), and from there, you'll probably have to catch another form of public transport or taxi on to your hotel.

Location
Around 19 Miles/30 km to the east of Bangkok
Nearby places
CentralwOrld (23.6 km)
Pantip Plaza (24 km)

Patpong Night Market (24 km)
Siam Paragon (24.2 km)
MBK shopping centre (24.6 km)

Bangkok Don Mueang Airport

Formerly Bangkok's main international airport, DMK, or Don Mueang Airport is the second most important flight station in the Thai city.

Before Suvarnabhumi Airport was opened in 2006, Don Mueang Airport was Bangkok's main flight hub. While it stopped business flights briefly when the new airport opened, giving it the airport code BKK, today Don Mueang Airport (DMK) is open and used by both local and (mainly regional) foreign flights.

Getting to Bangkok from Don Mueang Airport

There are several choices to reach the center of the Thai capital from DMK, fitting a wide range of prices and time constraints:

Taxi

Simple and quick, as long as you're happy speaking with drivers, the price varies on where your hotel is located in the city center. You shouldn't pay more than 350 THB (US$ 10), but remember there will be an additional 50 THB (US$ 1.40) airport charge and that customers pay for tolls. Taxis wait outside the arrivals halls - make sure your driver uses the meter!

Transfer help

The easiest and fastest way to get to your accommodation, pre-booking a car service to pick you up from Don Mueang Airport means you don't need to stress about finding a taxi and struggling with your Thai Bahts to pay.

Train

Cheap and lively, there is a train that connects Don Mueang with Hualamphong Train Station which costs no more than 10 THB (US$ 0.30). Trains leave every 1-1.5

hours between 4 am and 11:30 am and then roughly once an hour from 2 pm to 9:30 pm.

Bus

There are lots of different cars that leave the airport for Bangkok's main sights. Outside landings, buses run daily between around 7:30 am and 11:30 pm to the different BTS Skytrain stops and other important spots: bus A1 stops at BTS Mo Chit; A2 stops at BTS Mo Chit and BTS Victory Monument; A3 stops at Pratunam and Lumphini Park; and A4 stops at Th Khao San and Sanam Luang. They leave every half an hour and cost 50 THB (US$ 1.40).

Popular public bus lines (which you catch from the highway in front of the airport) include number 29, which runs 24 hours and goes to Hualamphong Train Station via Victory Monument BTS station; 59, also 24 hours, which stops near Th Khao San; and 538, which you can get to Victory Monument BTS station (runs 4 am to 10 pm). These cars cost about 20 THB (US$ 0.60).

Location

Around 17 miles / 28 km to the north of Bangkok

Nearby places

Chatuchak Weekend Market (14.2 km)

Pantip Plaza (19.7 km)

CentralwOrld (20.1 km)

Jim Thompson House Museum (20.3 km)

Siam Paragon (20.4

Entry and Exit Requirements

Each country or region sets its own entry and leave standards at its borders. If you fail to meet these standards for your location, your government will not be able to help you. The following information is given by Thai officials and is open to change without notice.

Passport

The entry prerequisites vary based on the visa type you are having for travel.

Prior to your trip, speak with your travel company regarding visa stipulations, as their expiration rules might be tougher than those required by the target country.

Ensure that your passport has at least six months of validity upon your arrival in Thailand.

Other Entry Requirements

Immigration officers at the Thai border may request to see a ticket for your return or onward trip, as well as proof of adequate funds to support you throughout your stay.

Failure to show these papers may result in denial of entry.

Entry Stamp

Obtain your entry stamp straight from a customs officer when entering Thailand. Avoid getting your visa, visa extension, or entry stamp through visa shops or travel providers within the country.

Passports that have been changed or carry fake visas and entry/exit stamps will be considered useless. Individuals found with such papers may face jail, fines, and removal, and might also be barred from future entry into Thailand.

Getting Around the City

There are a few different ways to get around Bangkok based on where you're living and where you're headed...

Skytrain

The Skytrain is an aerial train that is also known as **BTS**. At the time of writing, there are two lines, the Sukhumvit line (light green) and the Silom line (dark green). They're useful for dodging Bangkok's crazy traffic if you need to get around "new Bangkok", that is to say, the areas around Silom,

37

Sukhumvit, and Siam Square. Trains run frequently between 6 am and midnight, and ticket prices range from 15 THB (US$ 0.40) to 52 THB (US$ 1.50) or 140 THB (US$ 4) for a day pass. Ticket machines only accept coins, but the ticket offices will swap your notes for change.

Metro

Metro Bangkok's metro system (MRT) is also good for getting between the Sukhumvit or Silom areas to reach Hualamphong Train Station. It's cheap: tickets cost from 16 THB (US$ 0.50) to 42 THB (US$ 1.20) or 120 THB (US$ 3.40) for a one-day pass and again, the trains run frequently from 6 am to midnight. The popular Chatuchak Weekend Market is situated at Mo Chit station on the Sukhumvit BTS line and Chatuchak Park on the MRT line.

Boat

Bangkok is split in two by the Chao Phraya River, and the west side (formerly Thonburi) is still home to a pretty large canal system. One of the best ways (although not exactly the fastest) to visit places along the river bank, like the Grand Palace and Wat Pho Temple, is by boat. The main pier (Tha Sathon, or Central Pier) links with the Saphan Taksin BTS stop.

The Chao Phraya Express Boat (orange flag) leaves every 10 - 20 minutes between 6 am and 7 pm. Tickets cost 15 THB (US$ 0.40) and the boat stops at most important piers between Wat Rajsingkorn in the south of Bangkok, to Nonthaburi in the north.

The tourist boat (blue flag) runs from Central Pier to Phra Athit/Banglamphu Pier (number 13 on our map). It leaves every 30 minutes from 9:30 am to 5 pm and stops at 8 key sites on the way. Tickets cost 40 THB (US$ 1.10). The 150 THB (US$ 4.30) all-day ticket given by touts isn't usually worth it.

To cross the river, there are countless boats that run every few minutes all day and into the night, costing just 3 THB (US$ 0.10).

Taxi

Traveling around Bangkok by cab is surprisingly cheap - sometimes even more so than the Skytrain - plus, it's comfy and easy, and the drivers are usually really friendly. Taxis have to use their meters - if a driver refuses to do so, find a different cab! The meter starts at 35 THB (US$ 1) and trips to most places in central Bangkok will cost between 60 THB (US$ 1.70) to 90 THB (US$ 2.60). Remember that tolls are paid by the person. If you can't find a taxi ready to use the meter late at night, there are cab apps available: Grab Taxi and All Thai Taxi. Don't expect your driver to speak English. An address written in Thai is a good bet to ensure you'll get to the right place!

Grab

This new app-based cab business is a good way to get around Bangkok. trips are booked via a mobile application, and the journey has a set price meaning that you'll avoid fights and haggling with cab drivers. The program offers payment by card, or you can pay the driver in cash.

Tuk-tuks

Those famous motorized rickshaws are used by locals and tourists alike for short trips that aren't worth the cab fare. Tourists, however, are usually overpaid for these noisy and polluting trips! It's better to go at night when the smog isn't as bad (or to save this experience for another city!) and try and haggle the price down to 60 THB (US$ 1.70). Super cheap tuk-tuks are usually too good to be true and will take you to gem shops and massage parlors in the hope of some profit.

Bikes

While riding has gotten more and more popular in Bangkok over the years, it's still a bit of a minefield out there thanks to dangerous roads, crazy traffic, sweltering heat, and pollution (hopefully the bike trend will help that though!). If you feel the need to pedal around the Thai city, we suggest booking a Bike Tour with a guide who can show you the best places to ride.

Recommendations

We suggest using the metro and Skytrain as much as possible, not only to avoid traffic jams but also for your safety.

In Bangkok cabs can be even scary than in places like Cairo. In Bangkok the cars are new, and the drivers like to drive fast. And the majority of cabs don't have seatbelts in the back, so tourists are quite vulnerable. The same can be said too for the tuk-tuks in the city, where you're the only crumple zone…

Hotel

1. Khao San Road / Banglamphu

This is the main backpacker district of Bangkok, but at the same time it's the historical center of the city, where many of the famous attractions (like the Grand Palace) are located. You'll find budget hostels, historical guest houses, and hotels in this area.

43

HOTEL **Full House Khaosan (budget):**
This place is so close to the action of Khao San Road, but it's tucked away into a local alley, and remains quiet and friendly.

Nearest airport Don Mueang International Airport (DMK)

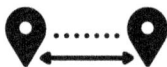

Distance to airport   20.37 km

2.77 kilometers from city center

Hygiene Plus

Located in heart of Bangkok

Check-in [24-hour]

Airport transfer

330 meters to Khaosan Road

Baan Chart Hotel (mid-range)
It's a decent choice for a mid-range priced hotel along Rambuttri, parallel to Khao San Road.

Nearest airport Don Mueang International Airport (DMK)

Distance to airport   20.06 km

0.5 kilometers from city center

(1.1km)Temple of emerald Buddha

Located in heart of Bangkok

Check-in [24-hour]

Airport transfer

200 meters to Khaosan Road

2. Chao Phraya Riverside /

Bangrak – The Chao Phraya Riverside is scenic, with good transportation options, and a mix of both luxury hotels and mid-range options. Great area for families because of the transportation options and mix of everything.

Glur Bangkok Hostel (budget) This is a new, clean, and modern hostel, near to the BTS.

Nearest airport Don Mueang International Airport (DMK)

Distance to airport   23.64 km

540 kilometers from city center

80meter to public transportation

Check-in [24-hour]

Airport transfer

Great Breakfast

Shangri-La (luxury)

A prime location and to the Shangri La standard, it's expensive, but a very nice hotel in Bangkok.

Nearest airport Don Mueang International Airport (DMK)

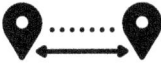

Distance to airport   23.52 km

5 kilometers from city center

Check-in [24-hour]

Airport transfer

220 meters to public transportation

Excellent room comfort & quality

Sparkling clean

Chatrium Riverside (luxury)

Experience the best Bangkok has to offer at Chatrium Hotel Riverside.5-star luxury hotel features breathtaking views

Nearest airport Don Mueang International Airport (DMK)

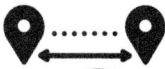

Distance to airport   24.72 km

5 kilometers from city center

Check-in [24-hour]

Airport transfer

960 meters to Asiatique-The Riverfront

Great Breakfast

Hygiene plus

3.Silom / Sathon

Silom and Sathon, located next to each other are the business financial districts of Bangkok, and very modern areas of town. The area makes a great base with food options and transportation.

Marvin Suites (mid-range)
For a budget and great value place to stay in Sathon, Marvin Suites is fantastic. The rooms are very spacious and it's the type of hotel that you'd feel comfortable staying at for one day or even a week or two.

Nearest airport Don Mueang International Airport (DMK)

Distance to airport   23.17 km

5 kilometers from city center

580 meter to public transportation

 Check-in [24-hour]

 Airport transfer

 Hygiene plus

 **Glow Trinity Silom (mid-range)**
This is a trendy type of hotel in a good location right in the heart of Silom.

 Nearest airport Don Mueang International Airport (DMK)

 Distance to airport 22.46km

 1 kilometers to city center

 located in heart of Bangkok

 Check In

 Great View

180 meter to public transportation

Great Breakfast

4. Siam / Pratunam

Siam and Pratunam are at the center of one of Bangkok's most intense shopping districts, with everything from modern malls to street shopping. Stay in Siam or Pratunam if you're serious about Bangkok shopping.

Lub d Siam Square (mid-range)
Lub d is a trendy modern hostel, located right across the street from MBK shopping mall.

Nearest airport Don Mueang International Airport (DMK)

Distance to airport 20.21 km

0.0 kilometers from city center

50 meter to public transportation

Located in heart of Bangkok

Check-in [24-hour]

Inside city center

Hygiene Plus

Amari Watergate (luxury)

Step outside Amari Watergate and you'll be in the midst of the Pratunam shopping district. Nice modern hotel, fantastic location.

Nearest airport Don Mueang International Airport (DMK)

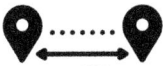

Distance to airport   20.21km

0.0 kilometers from city center

Check-in [24-hour]

Airport transfer

Located in heart of Bangkok

50 meters to public transportation

Hygiene plus

Inside city center

5.Sukhumvit

Sukhumvit Road is one of the major developed roads running through the heart of Bangkok, and it's home to many expats and international businesses and restaurants, but it remains local Thai at the same time.

St. James Hotel (mid-range)
This hotel is a little old, but well kept, and very comfortable and spacious

✈ Nearest airport
Suvarnabhumi Airport (BKK)

Distance to airport   19.89 km

300 meter to public transportation

Located in heart of Bangkok

Check-in [24-hour]

Airport Transfer

🏨 Pullman Bangkok Grande Sukhumvit (luxury)

Located near Asoke intersection, this is a nice business luxury hotel.

✈️ Nearest airport Don Mueang International Airport (DMK)

📍⋯📍 Distance to airport 18.65 km

0.5 kilometers from city center

Check-in [24-hour]

Airport transfer

Located in heart of Bangkok

Hygiene plus

Sparking Clean

Must-Visit Landmarks

Grand Palace and Wat Phra Kaew

IThe bright, amazing Grand Palace is definitely the most famous feature in Bangkok. It's one must-see sight that no visit to the city would be complete without. It was built in 1782 and for 150 years was the home of the Thai King, the Royal court and the executive seat of government.

The Grand Palace of Bangkok is a grand old dame indeed, that continues to have tourists in awe with its beautiful building and detailed detail, all of which is a proud salute to the creativity and craftsmanship of the Thai people. Within its walls were also the Thai war ministry, state offices, and even the bank. Today, the building remains the spiritual heart of the Thai Kingdom.

The Grand Palace
Within the palace complex are several impressive buildings including Wat Phra Kaew (Temple of the Emerald Buddha), which houses the small but famous and greatly adored Emerald Buddha that goes back to the 14th century.

The clothes on the Buddha are changed with the seasons by HM The King of Thailand – an important practice in the Buddhist calendar. Thai Kings stopped living in the palace around the turn of the 20th century, but the palace complex is still used to mark all kinds of other formal and important events.

Layout and direction of the Grand Palace

The palace complex, like the rest of Ratanakosin Island, is laid out very similar to

The palaces of Ayutthaya, the famous former capital of Siam which was raided by the Burmese.

The Outer Court, near the door, used to house government offices in which the King was personally involved, such as civil administration, the army and the budget. The Temple of the Emerald Buddha is set in one corner of this outer court.

The Central Court is where the home of the King and rooms used for conducting state business were located. Only 2 of the throne rooms are open to the public, but you'll be able to look at the fine detail on the faces of these amazing buildings.

The Inner Court is where the King's royal consorts and children lived. The Inner Court was like a small city completely occupied by women and boys under the age of puberty. Even though no royalty currently lives in the inner court, it is still completely closed off to the public.

Despite the closeness of the Grand Palace and Wat Phra Kaew, there's a clear difference in styles between the very Thai Temple of the Emerald Buddha and the more European inspired design of The Grand Palace (the roof being the main exception). Other features are Boromabiman Hall and Amarinda Hall, the original home of King Rama I and the Hall of Justice. Important tips about visiting the Grand Palace

A strict dress code applies. The Grand Palace, with the Temple of the Emerald Buddha, is Thailand's most holy spot. Visitors must be properly dressed before being given entry to the temple. Men must wear long pants and shirts with sleeves (no tank tops). If you're wearing shoes or flip-flops you must wear socks (in other words, no bare feet.)

Women must be similarly modestly dressed. No see-through clothes, bare shoulders, etc.

If you show up at the front gate poorly dressed, there is a booth near the door that can provide clothes to cover you up properly (a tip is needed).

Tickets to the Grand Palace are offered from 8.30am to 3.30pm and the price includes entry to Vimanmek Palace and Abhisek Dusit Throne Hall.

About Wat Phra Kaew

Wat Phra Kaew or the Temple of the Emerald Buddha (officially known as Wat Phra Sri Rattana Satsadaram) is viewed as the most important Buddhist temple in Thailand. Located in the historic heart of Bangkok, within the grounds of the Grand Palace, it enshrines Phra Kaew Morakot (the Emerald Buddha), the highly regarded Buddha figure carefully cut from a single block of jade. The picture can also be called Phra Putta Maha Mani Ratana Patimakorn and is in the meditation position. Its form is in the style of the Lanna school of the north.

Royal Reception Halls

Nowadays, its impressive interior is used for important formal events like coronations. It also includes the old chair, used before the western-style one currently in use. Visitors are allowed inside the large European-style welcome room or Grand Palace Hall (Chakri Maha Prasat).

Then there's the impressive Dusit Hall, rated as perhaps the best architectural building in this style, and a museum that has information on the repair of the Grand Palace, scale models and numerous Buddha images.

The Grand Palace in Bangkok Location: Na Phra Lan Road, Old City (Rattanakosin), Phra Nakhon, Bangkok 10200, Thailand

Open: Daily from 8.30am to 3.30pm

Wat Arun Temple

Wat Arun, locally known as Wat Chaeng, is a famous temple on the west (Thonburi) bank of the Chao Phraya river. It's easily one of the most beautiful temples in Bangkok, not only because of its riverfront location but also because the design is very different from the other temples you can visit in the Thai city. Wat Arun (nicknamed the 'Temple of Dawn') is partly made up of

62

colourfully painted towers and stands proudly over the water.

Wat Arun is almost exactly opposite Wat Pho, so it's very easy to get to. From Saphan Taksin boat pier you can take a barge that stops at Pier 8. From here, a small shuttle boat gets you from one side of the river to the other.

Visiting Wat Arun

We would suggest spending at least an hour visiting the temple. Although it's known as the Temple of the Dawn, it's absolutely stunning at sunset, especially when lit up at night. Even so, the best time to visit is early morning, before the crowds.

Given the beauty of the building and the fine workmanship, it's not strange that Wat Arun is viewed by many as one of the most beautiful temples in Thailand. The prang (spire) by the Chao Phraya is one of Bangkok's world-famous sights. The towering spire rises over 70 metres high, beautifully painted with tiny pieces of coloured glass and Chinese china put carefully into complex patterns.

You can climb the center prang if you wish – the steps are very steep but there's a fence to help with your balance. going up is as hard as going down! When you reach the highest point you can see the flowing Chao Phraya River and the Grand Palace and Wat Pho opposite. Along the base of this center tower are statues of Chinese troops and animals. Head into the ordination hall and you can enjoy a golden Buddha figure and the detailed paintings that cover the walls. Although Wat Arun is very popular for tourists, it's also an important place of worship for Buddhists. Make sure you dress properly or pick up one of the cover-ups that are available for rent near the door.

History of Wat Arun

Wat Arun was envisioned by King Taksin in 1768. It's thought that after making his way out of Ayutthaya, which was taken over by a

Burmese army at the time, he arrived at this temple just as dawn was breaking. He later had the temple restored and renamed it Wat Chaeng, the Temple of the Dawn. It used to be the home of the Emerald Buddha before the city and Palace was moved to the other side of the river. This can now be seen at the Grand Palace.

The center prang was widened during the rule of Rama III (between 1824 and 1851) and is now one of the most viewed places in Thailand. It was also Rama III who added the decorating of the towers with china so that they glimmer in the sunshine.

Location: 158 Wang Doem Road, Wat Arun, Bangkok Yai, Bangkok 10600, Thailand
Open: Daily from 8am to 5.30pm

Jim Thompson House

Jim Thompson House is the old home of the late James H.W. Thompson, an American businessman who spent over 30 years of his life to recovering Thai silk in the 1950s. The lovely garden-enclosed property sits on the bank of the Saen Saeb Canal and houses 6 traditional Thai teakwood houses moved from Ayutthaya and Ban Krua Silk Village. It's a museum and art centre showing Thompson's collection

66

of Asian antiques and Thai silk.

Highlights of Jim Thompson House in Bangkok

Jim Thompson House in Bangkok reflects Jim Thompson's life-long love and quirky design choices. The house's modest façade masks a beautifully decked entry hall, an unusual architectural feature in traditional Thai houses.

A smart lighting setup draws your eyes to 2 wall spaces showing a 17th-century standing Buddha and a hand-carved wooden figure. High above your head, a Belgian chandelier hangs from the ceiling, while Italian marble tiles cover the floor, punctuating heavy wood accents on the walls and indoors stairs.

Head upstairs to find a number of colorful wall hangings that Jim Thompson purchased from different Buddhist temples. These tell stories of the Buddha's previous and present lives, as well as his spiritual journey towards awakening. You'll also find a serious sandstone Buddha image guarding the door to the Thai kitchen, which shows Jim Thompson's collection of fine Benjarong porcelainware.

The eating room fills a 19th-century teakwood house, which Thompson moved from Ayutthaya. There's an eating table fashioned from 2 Chinese mahjong tables, with a blue-and-white china set put out as if dinner is about to be served.

With a 4-metre-high roof and 1 open-sided wall, Jim Thompson House's sitting room views the Saen Saeb Canal. The living room is built from a 100-year-old wooden house that once belonged to the Ban Krua Muslim community, who were the first makers of the Jim Thompson silk brand.

How to get to Jim Thompson House in Bangkok

Jim Thompson House is located in Siam, though it's closest to the National Stadium

BTS Skytrain Station. Once you exit from the train, take Exit 1 and turn right into Soi Kasemsan 2. Continue walking to the very end of the road, and the museum will be on your left-hand side.

Jim Thompson House in Bangkok Location: 6 Soi Kasemsan 2, Rama 1 Road, Wang Mai, Pathumwan, Bangkok 10330, Thailand
Open: Daily from 9am to 6pm

Explore the Floating Markets

The floating markets in Bangkok are one of the country's biggest draws. Although many of the rivers have been replaced by the road, their obvious charm makes them places worth visiting. There are many and you can spend your trip checking out these water markets in and around Bangkok on weekdays and weekends. Whether interested in grabbing the exclusive collections or just feel the vibe of these interesting markets, a

70

visit to any of these floating markets in Bangkok will surely enthrall you!

The ones that are not based in Bangkok are easily available in the least possible time. Make sure you do not miss these best Bangkok water markets while making your list of places to visit in Thailand.

Floating Markets In Bangkok And Near It

Most of the markets which are not centrally placed are in close proximity to Bangkok. They can be reached by boat which is the cheapest and most handy means of travel.

Khlong Lat Mayom – Local Food And More

Bang Nam Pheung– Known For Thai

Food Taling Chan Floating Market– Best Place For Massages

Damnoen Saduak Floating Market – A Vibrant Place To Shop At Amphawa

Floating Market Bangkok– Best Local Seafood

Tha Kha Floating Market – When Looking For Culinary Items

Bangkhla Floating Market – For The Quality Mangoes

Bangnoi Floating Market - Souvenirs And seafood

Bang Nok Kwaek – Old One Known For Thai Food

Muang Boran Floating Market – Witness The The Awe-Striking Replicas

Koh Kret Island Floating Market – A Great Place For Hanging Out

Kwan Riam Floating Market – Witness The Culture

Bang Khu Wiang Floating Market – For Farm -Fresh Cuisine

Wat Sai Floating Market – A Peek Into The Chinese Culture

Lam Phaya Floating Market – For Home-Cooked Delights

Bang Phli Floating Market – Oldest Floating Market In Bangkok

Khlong Lat Mayom Floating Market – Offers Variety Of Thai Food

Khlong Lat Mayom – Local Food And More
Just 20 kilometers from Bangkok is Khlong Lat Mayom, one of the best water markets in Bangkok. It's not as big as some of the other more well-known places like Damnoen

Saduak but that's what makes it so appealing. It's real and gives you an inside look at how people shop. You'll also find great food to savor on the floating market.

Famous for: is most famous for food. Try snakehead fish and the shrimps

How to reach: Take a BTS Skytrain to Bang Wa and then a cab ride to the floating market from Bang Wa. A straight cab will cost you around 200 Baht on one side.
Address:15 30/1 Bang Ramat Rd, Bang Ramat, Taling Chan, Bangkok 10170, Thailand
Timings: 7 AM – 5 PM (Sat-Sun)

Bang Nam Pheung: Known for Thai food Bang Nam Pheung is one of the best water markets in Bangkok. It's located on the edges and like Khlong Lat Mayom, it isn't as big and crowded as some of the more famous ones. One of the best ways to spend your time here is to eat on some of the best foods of Thailand. And there's plenty! Order a bowl of whatever gets your fancy from the many food sellers on boats. So, make sure to include this place in your floating market Thailand tour and have an exciting time!

Famous for: Gac Fruit, Mahk

How to reach: Taking a cab will cost you around 150-200 Baht. If you are coming from Sukhumvit, taking a boat ride to the floating market will be much cheaper.

Address: Bua Bueng Phatthana, Bang Kobua, Phra Pradaeng District, Samut Prakan 10130, Thailand

Timings: 8:30 AM – 5 PM (Sat-Sun)

Taling Chan Floating Market – Best Place For Massages

Taling Chan is set a few kilometers from Bangkok and although famous, it hasn't yet hit the crowd sizes of more business water markets. You can shop, eat, get a massage and get a look into the way of life here. Be sure to take a camera as the lively market offers more than enough picture possibilities. This is amongst the biggest floating market in Bangkok.

Famous for: Nursery plants, Thai food, and spas

How to reach: Public Transport is an easy choice. Get down at S6 Station, take a Chao Phraya Express Boat to Phra Pinklao Bridge Pier, and then Bus No. 79 from there to reach the floating market.

Address: 300 Soi Chak Phra 17, Khwaeng Khlong Chak Phra, Khet Taling Chan, Krung Thep Maha Nakhon 10170,

Timings: 8 AM – 6 PM (Sat-Sun)

Average Price: Boat costs are around 100 THB

Damnoen Saduak Floating Market– A Vibrant Place To Shop At One of the most famous floating markets in Thailand, Damnoen Saduak floating market is a great spot for tourists of all age groups. It's big and full of life. It's situated about 80 kilometers from the capital in Ratchaburi Province. Owing to its huge fame, Damnoen Saduak Floating Market near Bangkok can be very busy and touristy. However, it is certainly one of the

best places to visit in Bangkok.
If you're looking for a more laid-back place,
we suggest others like Khlong Lat Layom.
With no floating market, Bangkok entrance
fee, this is a good enough place to explore.

Famous for: Mini coconut pancakes, boat
noodles, flowers

How to reach: Located 100 km out of
Bangkok, the best way to reach here is
take a local tour.

Address: 9 Tambon Damnoen Saduak, Amphoe Damnoen Saduak, Chang Wat Ratchaburi 70130, Thailand

Timings: 7 AM – 4 PM (Everyday)

Average Price: 900 THB

Amphawa Floating Market Bangkok
-Best Local Seafood huge fameGet
Customized Quotes
After Damnoen Saduak, this is the most
popular floating market in Bangkok. Situated
about 50 kilometers away from the city, it

draws a large number of Thai tourists who come here to eat on delicious fish and shop.

When you're done eating and buying, hop on a longtail boat and explore the river. The price of visiting this floating market near Bangkok is about 50 THB for a shared tour and 500 THB for a solo trip.

Famous for: local seafood

How to reach: Amphawa is a 10-minute ride from Maeklong which has bus and train connections from Bangkok.

Address: Amphawa District of Samut Songkhram Province

Timings: 2-8 PM (Fri-Sun)

Experiencing Thai Cuisine 🍴

Culinary Delights in Bangkok

Eating Thai food is a big (and important) part of your trip in Bangkok and Thailand. Thanks to its exotic tastes and scents, Thai food is popular worldwide. A walk through the city's alleys often ends in a stop at a food stall, where you can enjoy grilled meats, fried rice, noodles, and hot soups at rather affordable prices.

If you prefer eating in a more cozy setting, Bangkok has plenty of places offering an extensive menu of classic Thai foods. Sample the very best of the city's local offers by turning to our guide to the best Thai food.

Spicy shrimp soup
Tom yum goong
Tom yum goong is a strong, delicious mix of fragrant lemongrass, chilli, galangal, kaffir lime leaves, onions, lime juice, and fish sauce. Containing juicy river shrimps and green mushrooms, this hot and sour soup is best paired with steamed white rice. Tom yum goong is a strong, delicious mix of fragrant lemongrass, chilli, galangal, kaffir lime leaves, onions, lime juice, and fish sauce. Containing juicy river shrimps and green mushrooms, this hot and sour soup is best paired with steamed white rice.

Spicy green papaya salad
Som tum
Som tum, or hot green papaya salad, comes from Thailand's north-eastern state of Isaan. Garlic, chillies, green beans, cherry tomatoes, and chopped raw papaya are crushed using a pestle and mortar, which release a sweet-sour-

spicy taste that's quite distinctive. Regional versions include peanuts, dry shrimp or salty crab into the mix. This food can be divisive, as some can't get enough of its taste, while others simply can't handle the heat.

Chicken in coconut soup
Tom kha kai

A mild, softer take on tom yum, tom kha kai adds hot chillies, thinly sliced young galangal, crushed shallots, stalks of lemongrass, and tender strips of chicken. The food also includes coconut milk to lessen the heat, before topping it off with fresh lime leaves. Like most Thai-style soups, you can pair your bowl of creamy tom kha kai with warmed rice.

Red curry
Gaeng daeng

Gaeng daeng is a savory red curry having meat, red curry sauce and smooth coconut milk, along with a topping of sliced kaffir lime leaves on top. Despite its striking colour, gaeng daeng is quite mild though you can request for fresh chilli if you're in the mood for spicy foods. Vegetarians or vegans can still enjoy this meal by asking the cook to change the meat with tofu.

Thai-style fried noodles
Pad Thai

Pad Thai is one of Thailand's most known meals. Fistfuls of small, thin or wide noodles, along with crunchy beansprouts, onion, and egg are stir-fried in a searing hot pan. The dish is also spiced with spices such as fish sauce, dried shrimp, garlic or shallots, red chilli, and palm sugar. Pad Thai usually includes seafood – especially fresh shrimp, crab or squid – but some places serve it with chicken, beef or pork. The stir-fried noodles are often served with a slice of lime wedge, crushed roasted peanuts, bean sprouts, and fresh herbs.

Fried rice
Khao pad

Fried rice, or khao pad, is often enjoyed for lunch in Bangkok. You easily boost up this simple dish of rice, egg and onion with your choice of items, from prawns, crab or chicken to tofu, basil or extra veggies.

Stir-fried basil and pork
Pad krapow moo

Pad krapow moo is a 1-plate Thai meal you can enjoy for lunch or dinner. Minced pork, holy basil leaves, big fresh pepper, pork, green beans, soy sauce, and sugar are stir-fried in a pan. The cooked mixture is piled onto a plate of hot white rice and topped with a fried egg (kai dao).

Green chicken curry
Gaeng keow wan kai

Gaeng keow wan kai gets its unique colour from green chillies, though items used are like most Thai soups. This green chicken soup includes coconut milk, cherry-sized eggplants, bamboo shoots, galangal, lemongrass, coriander and sweet basil. It tastes richer and sweeter than the standard tom yum, and goes well with flatbread or steamed rice.

Spicy beef salad
Yum nua

Yum nua is a cool Thai salad topped with strips of soft beef. It uses a spicy dressing made with lime juice, olive oil, soy sauce, ginger, garlic, fish sauce, and palm sugar. You can enjoy yum nua on its own, but having it with rice helps cut down the sour-sweet taste.

Stir-fried chicken with cashew nuts
Kai pad med ma muang

Kai pad med ma muang is simply stir-fried chicken with cashew nuts. This food also includes soy sauce, honey, onions, chillies, and pepper, as well as a range of veggies (usually chopped bell peppers or carrots).

There's dried chilli mixed in together with the chicken and cashew nuts, but it's hardly spicy. This dish is good for children or those who can't handle hot foods.

Popular Street Food Spots

Street food in Bangkok offers handy, delicious and cheap meals and it's one of the best ways to get in touch with the local culture. Even so, it can be a little frightening for visitors new to the cityStreet food is a unique part of the Bangkok experience. Wherever you go in the city, food stalls are plentiful and you will find a high number of them in busy places. Some street sellers work in groups, especially in local markets, which means

85

you can go to the same place every night and have a different choice of food. Some even open around the clock.

Bang Kho Laem
Guay Jub Mr. Joe (Mr Joe Crispy Pork)

A reputation for cooking the crispiest pork in town ensures a steady flow of customers at this third-generation restaurant with Chinese roots. Kuay jub is the highlight, a spicy rolled rice noodle soup with crispy pork and a long list of offal. The signature pork belly (with crunchy crackling) is also served solo with a dark sweet soy sauce (those with sensitive teeth should bite with care). Steamed pork, crab or prawn siu mai are good choices for a quick snack before the big event. Explore the surrounding streets to experience the charms of an old waterfront area before it's gentrified.

Best for: Crispiest pork belly in town and kuay jub (rolled rice noodle soup with crispy pork)

Address: 313/7 Chan Road, What Phraya Krai, Bang Kho Laem, Bangkok 10120
Kuay jub or a plate of crispy pork from 80 THB / 2.20 USDPrice:

Khlong San
Somsak Pu Ob

Munch on mud crabs and giant prawns cooked with glass noodles on the side of a busy old road in Bangkok's leather area. The chef at Somsak Pu Ob serves up precision food in memory of his father's heritage. Each pan is carefully watched over hot flames, flavored with black peppercorns and topped with green onion. Crab shells are served cracked for easy extraction of their sweet meat. Seafood is sourced from nearby Samut Sakhon province, and the noodles from a town in Thailand's west. It's no-frills eating at its best. There is a second Somsak Pu Ob branch close, but this is the original.

Best for: Crab or prawns steamed with glass noodles. Bangkok-style streetside dining.

Address: Charoen Rat Road Soi 1, Khlong Ton Sai, Khlong San, Bangkok 10600
Price: Steamed prawns with glass noodles from 290 THB / 7.90 USD; steamed crab with glass noodles from 310 THB / 8.35 USD. Cash only.

Mid-Sukhumvit
Mae Varee Mango Sticky Rice

This fruit shop gets local Nam Dok Mai peaches, preservative-free coconut milk and rice from independent farmers to make a perfect version of Thailand's flagship dish. It's no secret to locals and tourists alike, who get in line to buy in bulk. Sweet mangoes can be bought whole or newly sliced year round, while the sticky rice is naturally flavoured with coconut, butterfly pea or pandan plant. Small tubs of handmade mango or coconut ice cream and jelly line the fridge. The tiny store is located next to Thonglor station, which makes for a quick skytrain run. Alternatively, have cake brought to your room via an online app, morning to night.

Best for: Mango sticky rice, fresh mango or artisanal ice cream. Takeaway only.
Address:1 Thong Lo Road, Khlong Tan Nuea, Watthana, Bangkok 10110
Price: Mango sticky rice from 150 THB / 4.10 USD; peeled mango from 100 THB / 2.75 USD; mango ice-cream from 85 THB / 2.30 USD

Nhong Rim Klong

This backstreet shophouse serves sparkling fish in large amounts without the hype found elsewhere across town. While crab omelette may be the drawcard, mixed eggs with bits of softly cooked crab and boiled cabbage is a meal to dream about long afterwards. Huge wok-fried garlic prawns are another knockout alongside local fish, squid, hot soups, stews and fried rice. The kitchen works at a frantic pace to Thai techno, to keep up with a staggering number of orders. The eatery moved into a more roomy setting next door in early 2023 and local beer is also offered.

Best for: Calling all seafood lovers for crab omelette or wok-fried garlic prawns. Local shophouse experience.

Address: 51 Soi Ekkamai 23, Khlong Tan Nuea, Watthana, Bangkok 10110

Price: Signature crab omelette is 600 THB / 16.50 USD; stir-fries and curries from 200 THB / 5.50 USD

Phed Mark

What happens when two food writers, an Iron Chef, and a designer can't agree on who cooks Bangkok's best pad kaprao? They open a restaurant together dedicated to their best dish. As the name and burning logo suggest, heat is important ('phed' means spicy in Thai). There are five heat levels running from 'non spicy' to 'very spicy' – the latter is one for the brave. Legend has it there is also an off-menu choice that's double the heat of 'very spicy'. Choose from beef, pork, sour sausage, wagyu beef, squid or veggie, served with one of the prettiest fried duck eggs you'll

Best for: Stir-fried holy basil (pad kaprao) at various spice levels
Address:928 Sukhumvit Road, Phra Khanong, Khlong Toei, Bangkok 10110
Price: Stir-fried holy basil from 119-269 THB / 3.30-7.35 USD (depending on protein chosen)

Rung Rueang Pork Noodle

A short walk from Phrom Phong skytrain station, in an area where ramen shops mix with jacuzzi rooms and glamorous malls, lies one of Bangkok's most chaotic street food experiences. The small Rung Rueang Pork Noodle restaurant specialises in its named Thai pork noodles, served dry or with clear or hot tom yum soup topped with fish balls, chopped pork and liver. Staff move at speed, rapidly making bowls, blanching noodles and taking orders – a three step process suited to your tastes. If you think the morning trade is busy, wait for the lunchtime crush, where locals struggle for tables and a swarm of motorbike drivers eagerly await deliveries outside. Make sure to order an iced longan or plum juice to add a cooling touch to your meal. Note, Rung Reung Pork Noodle diner next door serves almost similar food by different family members to the original. Word has it there is a change in the feel of the noodles.

Best for: Thai pork noodles in spicy tom yum or clear soup

Address: 10/3 Soi Sukhumvit 26, Khlong Tan, Khlong Toei, Bangkok 10110

Price: Pork noodles from 50 THB / 1.40 USD

Best Restaurants in Thai

We all know that great Thai food can be found in the most simple shophouse or even by the roadside. But if you've come a long way and wish to treat yourself to something more sophisticated, here are great Thai places in Bangkok for a special treat.

Some of these places come with an expensive price but remember: this is a whole eating experience, with the service, setting and other small things that separate the great from

93

the good. Most of all, these places offer the chance to discover the true tastes of Thailand, all made by the most famous Thai cooks. It's not just about food; it's about cooking.

Issaya Siamese Club

Issaya is a 100-year-old house that sits proudly in the middle of a lush green yard. With its wooden porch and old-fashioned stairs, it quickly sets a romantic mood, making it a great place for duo eating.
This is not another pretty tourist place: Thais, expats and the few visitors who make the effort to find it are united – the combined charm of a heritage house, excellent service and the famous culinary flair of Chef Ian Kittichai makes Issaya Siamese Club an outstanding restaurant.
Location: 4 Soi Si Akson, Thung Maha Mek, Sathorn, Bangkok 10120, Thailand
Open: Daily from 11.30 am to 2.30 pm and from 6 pm to 10.30 pm

Bo.Lan Restaurant

Recognised for many years as one of the best Thai restaurants in Bangkok, Bo.Lan is not your everyday local spot. This is the kind of place to bring your discerning friends or for when you want to impress guests who think they've 'tried it all before'.

The name 'Bo.Lan' comes from the 2 cooks – 'Bo' (Duangporn Songvisava) and 'Dylan Jones' – who were both inspired by and worked under the direction of Michelin-starred chef David Thompson at Nahm London.

Location: 24 Sukhumvit Soi 53, Khlong Tan, Watthana, Bangkok 10110, Thailand

Open: lunch: Thursday–Sunday from midday to 2.30 pm, dinner: Wednesday – Saturday from 6 pm to 10.30 pm (closed on Mondays and Tuesdays)

Sala Rim Naam at the Mandarin Oriental

Sala Rim Naam at the Mandarin Oriental Bangkok mixes all the essential elements to offer one of the best romantic Thai eating experiences in the city. This isn't an easy thing to achieve, with so many great places around town. Sala Rim Naam works thanks to its great setting by the riverside – not 2 metres from the water, but right next to your table! Another element is the famous Mandarin Oriental service and, of course, all these would be useless without the key part of a truly great place: the food.

Location: Mandarin Oriental Bangkok, 48 Oriental Ave, Khlong Ton Sai, Bang Rak, Bangkok 10500, Thailand

Open: Daily from 11.30 am to 2.30 pm and from 7 pm to 10 pm

Nahm Restaurant

Nahm offers Thai food made according to old recipes with a focus on how the tastes and textures of high quality ingredients interact together. It's regularly ranked among the best places in the world, and with a Michelin-star chef at the head

Whether you are a longtime visitor to Bangkok or it's your first time eating traditional Thai food, Nahm will both surprise and please you with fantastic meals

Location: Como Metropolitan Hotel Bangkok, 27 Sathon Tai Rd, Thung Maha Mek, Sathorn, Bangkok 10120, Thailand

Open: Monday–Friday from midday to 2 pm and from 6.30 pm to 11 pm, Saturday-Sunday from 6.30 pm to 11 pm

Saffron at Banyan Tree

Fantastic views, delicious food, a warm setting and helpful service come together at Saffron Thai restaurant, ensuring that every guest gets a true taste of Thailand. All are treated with Banyan Tree's special style of kindness.

The restaurant is split over 2 stories, high above the city on the 52nd floor of the Banyan Tree Hotel on Sathorn Road. The closest stop is Lumphini MRT, but we suggest taking a cab; the hotel is well known

to taxi drivers. There's a smart casual dress rule at Saffron restaurant, so no flip-flops, shorts, sportswear or open shoes for guys.
Location: 21, 100 S Sathon Rd, Thung Maha Mek, Sathorn, Bangkok 10120, Thailand
Open: Daily from 11.30 am to 2.30 pm and from 6 pm to 10.30 pm

Restaurants in Bangkok Chinatown

If you're brave enough and forget everything you thought you knew about food, Chinatown will surprise you. Street food is always fun and tourists seem to enjoy mixing with locals to experience something traditional. Yaowarat is famous for its very popular food stalls set on the most impractical sidewalks, not to mention the iffy health conditions. And yet, each plastic chair is

99

filled and a queue is calmly standing by, trying not to get hit by tuk-tuks and bikes going by.

There's also a small range of indoor restaurants complete with menus in English, including amazing tea rooms with hundreds of types of tea and spots serving fusion food with Asian tastes. Bangkok Chinatown is a journey, and the sooner you find it the better. Also, note that the Chinatown food scene mostly comes alive around sunset!

Rut & Lek Seafood

Lek & Rut Seafood in Chinatown is a testament to Bangkok being a city of extremes, especially when it comes to food. This Chinatown restaurant serves great food in the most odd setting you could dream of for a nice dinner: a busy intersection of Bangkok Chinatown. Having dinner at Lek & Rut is the best way to experience the way of life and culinary open-mind of Bangkok. You need to forget everything you know and just go with the flow – it's a fun and interesting experience.

Nothing separates Lek & Rut Seafood from its nearby street carts, except that it's now famous, and of course popular. It's always packed and yet people calmly wait for a seat, standing wherever possible on the busy road. Don't expect plates, silverware and air conditioning here. Set on the narrow pavement of the incredibly busy Yaowarat Road, it's a secret how cars, bikes and by-passers manage to get past without hitting an eating table.

Location: Phadung Dao Rd, Samphanthawong, Bangkok 10100, Thailand

Open: Daily from 5.30pm to 2am

T & K Seafood

T & K Restaurant on Yaowarat road is busy every single evening come rain or shine. Just like many other famous restaurants in the area, it's not about fancy design and

glamorous decor, but about great simple food

and the rural charm of eating on the ground of a busy street.

The outdoor area is the most famous but as it's permanently packed you can eat inside or even upstairs with air-conditioning. Even so, the room is bare with the usual plastic chairs and iron tables, and the cleaning applies no further than the top of your table, which by street-food standards is all you need. T & K is dedicated to seafood – once you've tried their amazing whole steamed or deep-fried fish served with different types of sauce, huge grilled prawns, crabs, great seafood soups and delicious shells, then you'll know why people queue up outside, even in the rain!
Location: 49-51 Phadung Dao Rd, Samphan-thawong, Bangkok 10100, Thailand
Open: Daily from 4pm to 2am

Red Rose Restaurant at Shanghai Mansion Hotel

Red Rose Restaurant gives a 1930s Shanghai restaurant idea where you can have a real touch of flare to your food. You can find it on the second floor of the Shanghai Mansion Bangkok Boutique Hotel. The decor is simply wonderful with a circular cast-iron stairs, traditionally cushioned seats and period touches such as gramophones and old furniture.

The fact that Red Rose restaurant looks onto Yaowarat Road means it is central to all the sites and shops of Chinatown and makes a great place for lunch or dinner.

Location:481 Yaowarat Rd, Samphanthawong, Bangkok 10100, Thailand
Open: Daily from 10am to 11pm

Krua Porn Lamai

Krua Porn Lamai is a normal street food shack for those who enjoy eating like locals, and by that, we mean 'really local'. The simple cooking station is on one side of the street and the tables are on the other, lined against a sooty wall so the waiters have to constantly cross the busy street with boiling hot plates.

Despite its shabby appearance, and just like most restaurants in Bangkok Chinatown, Krua Porn Lamai is always full, but for the first-timer, it takes a bit of courage to pick this place (don't expect an illustrated English menu, all you have is a brief written in Thai above the cart).

Famous for its sizzling hoy tod (mussels and bean sprouts eggs served on a cast iron plate) and for its even more hot rad na. Rad na is a mix of crabs, squid, chicken and veggies also brought on an iron dish. Other suggested favorites are guay taew kua krob (stir-fried crispy noodles) and taro kua (stir-fried taro snacks).

Location:64 Plaeng Nam Rd, Samphanthawong, Bangkok 10100, Thailand
Open: Daily from 6pm to 2am

Kuay Jab Nai Huan

Kuay Jab Nai Huan is one of Yaowarat road all-time faves... This small stall only serves one dish and is packed non-stop from 6 in the evening to late at night. Kuay Jab is made of large rolled rice noodles with crispy pork belly, sometimes with guts and most importantly served in a very very spicy clear soup, with costs starting at around 40 baht.

It's so famous you'll certainly have to queue calmly, standing in this incredibly busy intersection. Or, if you're lucky, they might take you further down the lane to set a table up just for you, in the middle of nowhere.
Location: 4 Yaowarat Rd, Chakkrawat, Samphanthawong, Bangkok 10100, Thailand

Beyond the Tourist Trail

Hidden Gems and Local Hangouts

First-timers to Bangkok often visit the city's historic sites and popular places during their trip. All must-see sites are popular for good reason so yes, you should see them at least once if only to tick them off the list.

But if you're a return visitor, you'll find plenty of secret gems that only locals and knowledgeable outsiders know about. In a city so full of differences and surprises, we've formed an affinity for lesser-known placesqes

Artist's House

The Artist's House is an art gallery filling a centuries-old wooden house in Thonburi. It's most famous for holding traditional Thai puppet shows, where intricately-made dolls are controlled by artists dressed in black. A pier going to the gallery is lined with shops, cafes, local restaurants, and a temple. You can also spot many odd and human-sized figures painted in white, red and black sitting by the water.

Location: Soi 28, Wat Kuhasawan, Thonburi, Bangkok 10160, Thailand
Open: Daily from 10am to 6pm

Steve Cafe & Cuisine

Steve Cafe & Cuisine is tucked away on the riverside, far from busy streets, with no easy entry and with no big signs. Opened in 2012, this Thai restaurant offers a relaxed setting with a cool river breeze and helpful staff to finish the whole easy-going experience. No dishes are cooked in advance, so some dishes can take some time to make and when the restaurant is full (which is every night), service can be a bit slow.

Location: 68 Sri Ayuthaya Road, Soi Sri Ayuthaya 21, Wachira Phayaban, Dusit, Bangkok 10300, Thailand

Open: Daily from 11am to 10.30pm

Bang Nam Pheung Market

Bang Nam Pheung Market is one of the most genuine markets near Bangkok. Mostly visited by locals, it's a chance to discover and taste local foods, sweets, and odd fruits. The general mood is relaxed and nice. People are very friendly, especially if you're keen to taste interesting-looking foods at the market. Rows of low tables are set along the stream under a long and wooden roof.

Location: Bang Nam Phueng, Phra Pradaeng, Samut Prakan 10130, Thailand

Open: Friday– Sunday from 8am to 2pm (closed from Mondays to Thursdays)

Double Dog Tea Room

Double Dog Tea Room in Bangkok's Chinatown serves a choice of fine teas and Chinese cakes with all the pride and ceremony of a traditional tearoom. This air-conditioned shophouse on Yaowarat serves as a casual hangout after a day of exploring the endless lanes of sellers and vendors. For newbies to the world of tea, the menu is helpful and easy to read, with separate parts on different tea types and locations. At Double Dogs Tea Room, there are unique teas from China, Taiwan, Sri Lanka, and Japan.

Location: 406 Yaowarat, Sampanthawong, Bangkok 10100, Thailand
Open: Tuesday–Thursday from 1pm to 9pm, Friday–Sunday from 1pm to 10pm (closed on Mondays)

Museum of Contemporary Art in Bangkok

The Museum of Contemporary Art in Bangkok (MOCA) houses a comprehensive collection of modern painting and sculpture

in Thailand. A must for any lover of art, the 5-storey museum contains over 800 pieces of art collected by communications magnate Boonchai Bencharongkul and showcase the development of Thai fine art since the introduction of modern western concepts. The Museum of Contemporary Art Bangkok is in Chatuchak, about 6.5 km north of the Mo Chit BTS Skytrain Station.
Location: 99 Kamphaeng Phet 6 Rd, Chatuchak, Bangkok 10900, Thailand
Open: Tuesday–Sunday from 10am to 6pm (closed on Mondays)

Shopping Mall

The best places to go shopping in Bangkok go far beyond a stroll in a mall or a morning spent browsing a market. Shopping in Bangkok is a day-and-night activity that runs alongside with the best in the west, while also giving a taste of the cultural uniqueness of the east. Work your way through these entirely different shopping experiences, and you'll soon come to understand why Bangkok is such a famous retail hub.

111

Bangkok Shopping Malls
Everywhere

In a city blessed with some of the world's most sumptuous malls, how do you choose? Do you want bargains galore? Go to MBK Center. After the biggest and most trendy? CentralWorld is your ticket. How about classy? Make your way to The Emporium. Of course, if glamour makes you go wobbly at the knees, you may already have found EmQuartier, Icon Siam, and Siam Paragon – the epitome of high-class Bangkok shopping malls.

Chatuchak Weekend Market
Chatuchak

The market of all markets, Chatuchak Weekend Market is the ideal outdoor Bangkok shopping experience. You will be amazed by its vast size, but perhaps even more so by the amazing variety of items. Stumble across anything from vinyl records and beads, to pieces of armour and Buddhist pictures. Haggling is allowed – just do so nicely. Possibly the most exciting, hectic and lively shopping experience that can be had anywhere in the world.

Night Market
Khao San - Patpong - Rod Fai Market

In most towns, nighttime means closure time for most shopping shops. Not so, here in Bangkok. Come dusk, Khao San Road teems with scruffy travel wear, while Patpong Market's tarpaulin-covered stalls – each filled with counterfeits or exotica – don't even kick into life until the area's office workers are tucked up in bed. Just 2 examples, among several, of Bangkok's love affair with the after-dark shop.

Asiatique The Riverfront
Riverside

Asiatique: The Riverfront has successfully united 2 of the most popular shopping experiences in the city: a night market and a mall. Just 10 minutes downriver from the

Saphan Taksin BTS Skytrain Station, this huge model warehouse complex has more than over 1,500 shops and 40 restaurants. You can also watch a Muay Thai fight or entertainment show in the nights.

Icon Siam Shopping Mall
Riverside

Icon Siam Mall is often called the "Mother of All Malls" in Bangkok, with 500 shops and 100 restaurants from more than 30 different countries. Developed by the same tycoons behind Siam Paragon and EmQuartier, Icon Siam offers high-end brands, an indoor floating market, an art center, show space, and a beautiful waterfront site with views of downtown Bangkok.

Nightlife

If you visit Bangkok and you plan to party, then Sukhumvit Road will be the centre of your world. This main road holds most of the best clubs and bars that the city has to offer, not to mention the famous red-light areas of Soi Cowboy and Nana Plaza.

Soi 11 is always busy and sure to be pumping into the early hours while the Thong Lor area (Soi 55) gets a more socialite crowd, with an even split between Thais and foreigners. The BTS Skytrain's Sukhumvit Line goes directly over Sukhumvit Road making this place the most handy for tourists to experience this adult's playground.

Soi Cowboy

At first sight, Soi Cowboy looks like a dream land of bright pink lights. But dreams here become real for all those looking for the dark side of Bangkok's nighttime culture: namely, go-go bars. This red-light district has a more laid-back, carnival-like feel to it than other famous go-go districts such as Patpong or Nana Plaza.

The lively landscape is made mainly of middle-aged expats, Japanese and western tourists, and of course a lot of sexily dressed girls. There are more than 20 bars lined one next to the other, each following the same formula of a central stage, loud music and scantily clad dancers. Typically, bars here are open from 8pm to 2am.

between Thais and foreigners. The BTS Skytrain's Sukhumvit Line goes directly over Sukhumvit Road making this place the most handy for tourists to experience this adult's playground.

Location: 23 Sukhumvit Rd, Khlong Toei, Watthana, Bangkok 10110, Thailand

Octave

Octave Rooftop and Lounge is more than a place for watching the sunset or having a nice meal. Sukhumvit Road in Bangkok waited a long time for its very own rooftop bar, and then finally Octave came along and showed the rest of them how it should really be done. No rooftop bar in the city has a 360-degree view of Bangkok that beats this, and the top floor of this 3-level venue is among the greatest spots in the city for a party. The Octave Rooftop Bar journey starts on the 45th floor of the Marriot Hotel Sukhumvit, a 3-minute walk from Thong Lor Skytrain Station.

Location: 45th-49th Floor, Bangkok Marriott Hotel Sukhumvit, 2 Sukhumvit Soi 57, Bangkok 10110, Thailand

Levels

Levels Club & Lounge is a place with 3 separate party zones housed in one linked area and offers a great alternative to the already rocking nighttime scene on Sukhumvit Soi 11. Combining parts of a tiered bar, classy lounge, and a box-like dancing room that has one of the best sound systems in the city, Levels covers a lot of musical ground and tries to provide a little something for everyone.

Occasionally, they charge an entry fee for special events or on nights with foreign DJs, but it's free entry most of the time.

Location:
6th Floor, Aloft Bangkok Sukhumvit 11, 35 Sukhumvit Rd, Khlong Toei Nuea, Watthana, Bangkok 10110, Thailand

Beam Nightclub

Beam Nightclub Bangkok is one of the liveliest dance places in the city, bringing underground house and techno music to Bangkok's bass heads. The music policy is closely sticking to the 'cooler' parts of the dance music scene so don't expect to hear singing EDM tracks. The music style you're most likely to hear is minimal and deep tech-house in the bare, dark main room that is more reminiscent of European dance clubs than the glitzy and glamorous style of parties often chosen by Thais. The VOID Acoustics sound system at Beam Club Bangkok is incredibly good, as is the LED laser and light show.

Location: 72 Soi Sukhumvit 55, Klongton Nua, Watthana, Bangkok 10110, Thailand

Nana Plaza

Nana Plaza is Bangkok's naughtiness central, located on Sukhumvit Soi 4. Notorious for its racy themed go-go bars, there are 3 storeys of eye-popping activity all focused around a square-shaped central atrium.

Unlike at the better-known Soi Cowboy or Patpong, Nana Plaza is a more 'adult' scene. That means no families, no markets and few curious tourists. It's still worth a look if you are searching for an exotic visual experience, and a story to talk about when back home, but be prepared to be shocked

Location: 3-1 Sukhumvit Road, Khlong Toei, Bangkok 10110, Thailand

Popular Scams

Bangkok is a great place to visit, blessed with a very high level of safety compared to any other major towns in the world. However, just like anywhere, some shady individuals specialise in the art of taking advantage of new tourists. Despite their tricks being rather clear, people who are a bit lost, a bit jet-lagged, and maybe also a bit naive still fall into the bad guys' net every single day. It happens to the best of us, from

SCAM ALERT

time to time.

However, informed is forearmed and knowing what to look out for (and adding a good amount of common sense) will help you avoid the more common scams. In all the following cases, the trends are similar and a simple "No, thank you" is all you need to say

The "Grand Palace is closed today" scam

This is one of the best-known scams and yet dozens of people fall for it every day. You're walking around one of the Bangkok sites, let's say the Grand Palace (Wat Phra Kaew) or nearby Wat Pho, when a happy Thai stranger approaches, asking where you're from. Following a little small talk, the guy will ask where are you going and by doing so will quickly analyse who you are and if this is your first time in Thailand. If it is, the story starts. "Oh, you want to see the Grand Palace today? Such bad luck – it's closed for the whole day for a special royal event!"

Of course, this kind of scam happens far from the gate, making sure you can't see the huge crowd coming in. Instead, he will offer to show you other great temples around Bangkok in his tuk-tuk for only 20 to 40 baht, and he can even be your guide to a wonderful day you'll never forget. In a way, he is right about that.

As you are very upset to have driven all the way to find the Grand Palace closed, you'll feel pleased that this guy happens to be on your path. He'll take you on a fun tuk-tuk ride to another temple, which will probably be very nice, boosting your level of trust. In this temple, you'll 'accidentally' meet another 'honourable' man who will welcome you and ask if you heard about this great government promotion (called Thai Gem Expo or similar names), which allows tourists to buy duty-free gems and stones at very low cost. Now here is how the trick works for him.

1) He will stop at a 'Authorised' TAT (Tourism Authority of Thailand) office just in case you would like to take advantage of those great travel deals that are just finishing today. What a chance! Of course, the agency is in no way related to the TAT, and the deal doesn't end today... it's not even a deal since you'll probably pay more than in any other agency.

2) He'll stop at the above-mentioned jewel shop where someone will show you some beautiful stones, maybe even including some real ones. But because the offer is duty-free, the gems you are buying will have to be shipped straight to your home address. The stones may really arrive, but the market value of what you'll get will be ridiculously cheap.

From this moment onward, the nice happy guy will become increasingly pushy, trying by any means to make you buy tickets or packages until you do, then will suddenly disappear while you are visiting the next temple.

How to recognise the scam:

While it's very normal for people to help you when you do need help, it's very suspicious when someone offers you help when you don't need it. A friendly unknown Thai guy speaking English a little too well, especially near a tourist area, is usually a pro. He often carries a map and an umbrella because it's hot for him to be out there all day long.

The Tuk-Tuk scam

Similar to the Grand Palace scam, but in a more direct manner: Tuk-tuks stopped in front of sites, hotels, shopping malls and other touristy places ask for a ridiculous price for a short distance and/or serve you lines like, "Can you please help me get free gasoline by just stopping few minutes at the gem shop? You don't even have to buy something, you can just look around and leave."

125

Because you are a very nice person, you won't mind, just to do your chance act of kindness for the day. Thanks to the high-pressure sales methods, most people end up getting something. In the best case, the driver will get his fee; in the worst case, you buy a superb piece of useless coloured glass.

How to recognise the scam:
Avoid tuk-tuks parked near shops and hotels or refuse any stop on the way to your destination.

The Patpong scam
The good old Patpong scam still works just a smoothly as it did over 20 years ago, taking advantage of naughty interest. As you walk through the red-light area of Patpong, trying to decide which go-go bar looks the least shady, a man approaches you with "The Menu". This is a list of all the fun acrobatics you'll be lucky enough to watch if you follow him (the famous ping pong show is one of the tamer examples). Of course, you are curious

and you have every right to be. You think this is probably as good a chance as any to take your walk on the wild side, especially when the guy adds, "If you no like, you no pay".

Now, this is when you can start being suspicious. The bar is usually upstairs and has no name... just a plain door opening on a small, shady place with a small bunch of girls, some of whom will join you when you take a seat. You order a beer and, by doing so, you're already done for the day! The girls will push for a lady drink. Want to ask how much a girl drink cost? "No problem! Same yours!" – of course, you have no idea how much yours cost in the first place, but you'll find out soon enough. Some kind of show starts, possibly one from "The Menu". Just 1 tiny trick and already you'll be pressed to tip generously.

At that point, most people figure out something isn't quite right and consider leaving. "Check please! 2,000 baht, sir", which is the price for your beer and some lady drink you can't really remember getting. Of course, you'll challenge that bill, but the big guy next to the door will give you "The Look" and maybe a small discount, but pay the bill, you will!

How to recognise the scam:

Any guy approaching you with a dirty menu is suspicious. All the bars at ground level in Patpong have set prices for drinks, while any placed above is possibly a scam. If you are asked to 'go upstairs', just tell them you changed your mind and suddenly feel like having ice cream instead.

The taxis parked in front of your hotel scam

This is an easy scam to spot and easy to avoid once you are aware of it. In front of every 4- and 5-star hotel, there are always 2 or 3 cabs stopped all day long, with taxi drivers hanging around, obviously not desperate to pick up any people from the street. These cabs might appear to be given to the hotel, but they are in no way a service offered by your hotel.

Instead, they'll spot hotel guests looking for a cab and kindly offer their service. Since they are always parked here, you think that's convenient, so you hop in and off you go. That's when you realise that the meter is off, so you kindly ask to have it turned on. At that point, the driver will make an offer, something like 500 baht to the airport (instead of the normal 300 to 350), but will never switch on his meter. As you are already rolling, it's hard to ask the cab to stop, especially since your bag is in the boot.

How to avoid the scam:
It's always better to flag a taxi down from the street but, if one isn't available, insist on the meter being switched on before you start rolling. If all else fails, use a ride-hailing app like Grab.

The khlong scam

A nice Thai man will approach you in the street and will start the same small talk that kicks off the Grand Palace scam. These guys always seem to have a story about your country and always know a couple of words in your language. They also seem to know all the football players from every country, so if you are a football fan, you just found yourself a buddy who'll happily hit on that nail. The man will offer you to ride his friend's longtail boat to go around the famous khlongs (canals) of Bangkok for a ridiculously low price.

The tour is real and actually very nice, so enjoy it – you might as well get something good out of the day before the scam ruins what's left of it! Your guide might even stop at a riverside bar and kindly offer you a soft drink. So far so good, and as the ride is about to end you think how lucky you have been today!

As you near the dock, the engine stops 200 metres from the pier and your new friend will ask for an additional 1,000 baht – or more – for the cost of the boat ride. No matter what you say and how much you fight, the boat won't get any closer to the pier. You will, of course, pay because the option is swimming back to the pier with your expensive camera and smartphone, neither of which are worth less than 1,000 baht.

How to avoid scam:

Don't trust people approaching you in the middle of nowhere with too good motives. Just smile and decline. If you want to explore the khlongs by boat, book a trip with a tour company or at the docks. Note that happy guys might try to approach you at the pier as well, but always buy your own ticket at the desk.

Conclusion

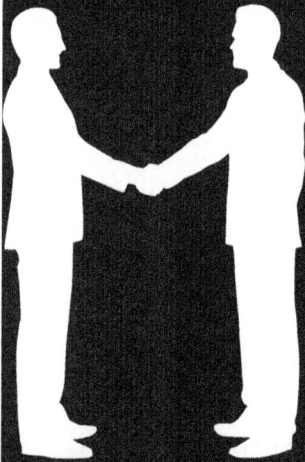

As we draw the curtains on this narrative adventure, I offer my deep thanks for joining this literary escapade. Your choice to explore these pages has knitted you into the fabric of stories, travels, and ideas. Whether you wanted information, pleasure, or simply a brief break, remember that within the vast worlds of words, you've found a treasure trove of fantasy. As you close this chapter, may the memories of the tales stay, and the knowledge gained join you on your next trip, whether it be within these pages or beyond. Happy reading, fellow traveler! 132

Travel Journal

Pack your stuff

Weekly

Monday	Tuesday	Wednesday	Thursday
Friday	Saturday	Sunday	Monday

Clothing

- ◯ T-shirt/Tops
- ◯ Undergarments
- ◯ Sweater or jacket
- ◯ pants/shorts/skirts
- ◯ ....
- ◯ ....
- ◯ ....

Hygiene

- ◯ Toothbrush
- ◯ Toothpaste
- ◯ Shampoo
- ◯ Soap or body wash
- ◯ ....
- ◯ ....
- ◯ ....

Essentials

- ◯ Identification
- ◯ Cash
- ◯ Passport
- ◯ ....
- ◯ ....
- ◯ ....

Tech

- ◯ Smartphone and charger
- ◯ Power bank
- ◯ Camera
- ◯ ....
- ◯ ....
- ◯ ....

My Expenditure

Keep track of your spending

Amount	Description	Date

Memories

My Ticket

My Experience

....
....
....
....
....

My Notes

....
....
....
....

My Rating

Travel Guide

From ....

Were to go

....
....
....
....
....
....

Add map

Hotspot

Restaurant

Accomodations

Top deal

....
....
....
....
....

Attraction

....
....
....
....
....

My Favorite Songs

Do you have a song that reminds you of your trips?
write them down

My Sketches

Set your mind in the winds and
draw your moment

Departure

Ticket	Hours	Date	Passenger
	From		To
	Seat		Gate

Arrival

Ticket	Hours	Date	Passenger
	From		To
	Seat		Gate

Local Friend

Remember the people you have met

Draw them

Memories

Memories

Keep in touch

Name _____

Phone _____

Address _____

Email _____

Travel Album

Stick your photo here

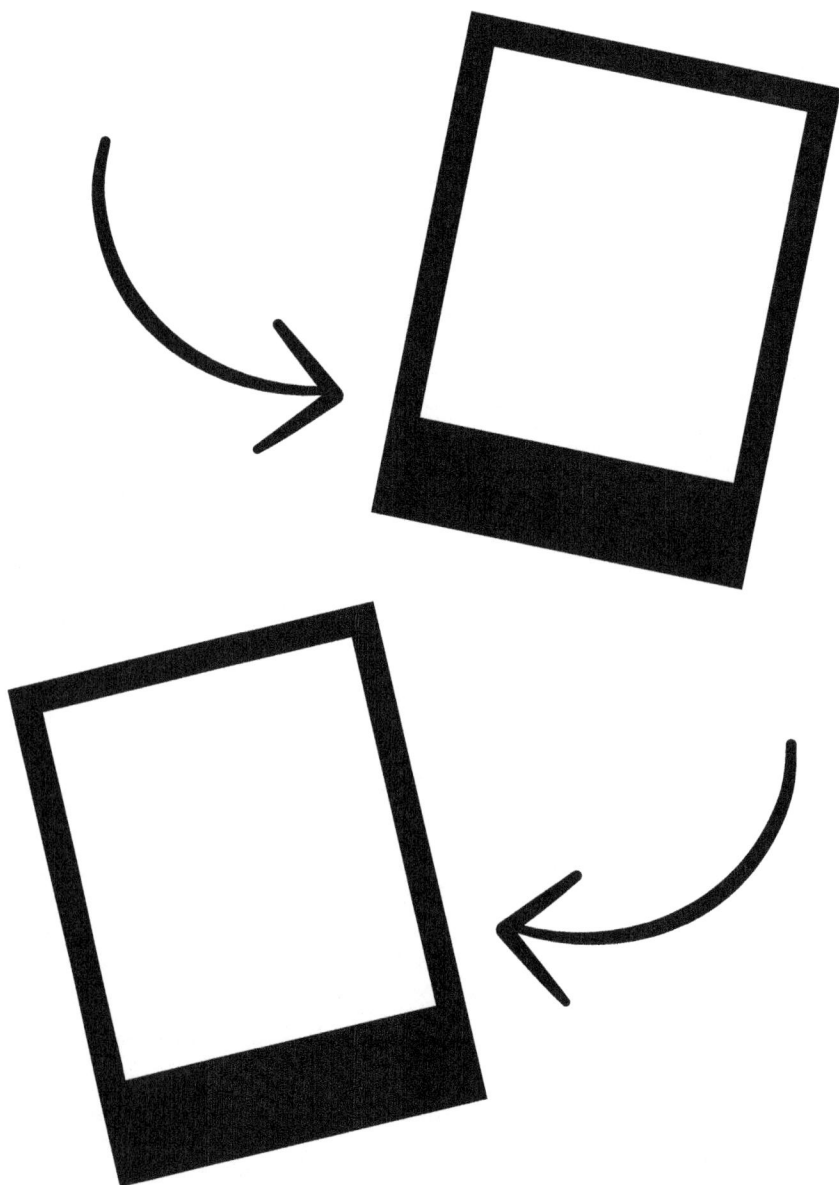

Places to visit

Create your perfect Trip

Khlongs of Thonburi	Soi Rambuttri	Wat Mahathat
Grand Palace	Wat Arun	Wat Pho
Chatuchak Weekend Market	Jim Thompson House	Khao San Road
Lumpini Park	MBK Center	Chinatown (Yaowarat)
Erawan Shrine	Asiatique The Riverfront	Bangkok Art and Culture Center
Siam Paragon	Ratchada Rot Fai Night Market	Benjasiri Park
The Golden Mount (Wat Saket)	Museum of Contemporary Art (MOCA)	Thip Samai Pad Thai
Flow House Bangkok	Terminal 21	Floating Markets

Departure

Time	To	Gate	Day

Arrival

Time	To	Gate	Day

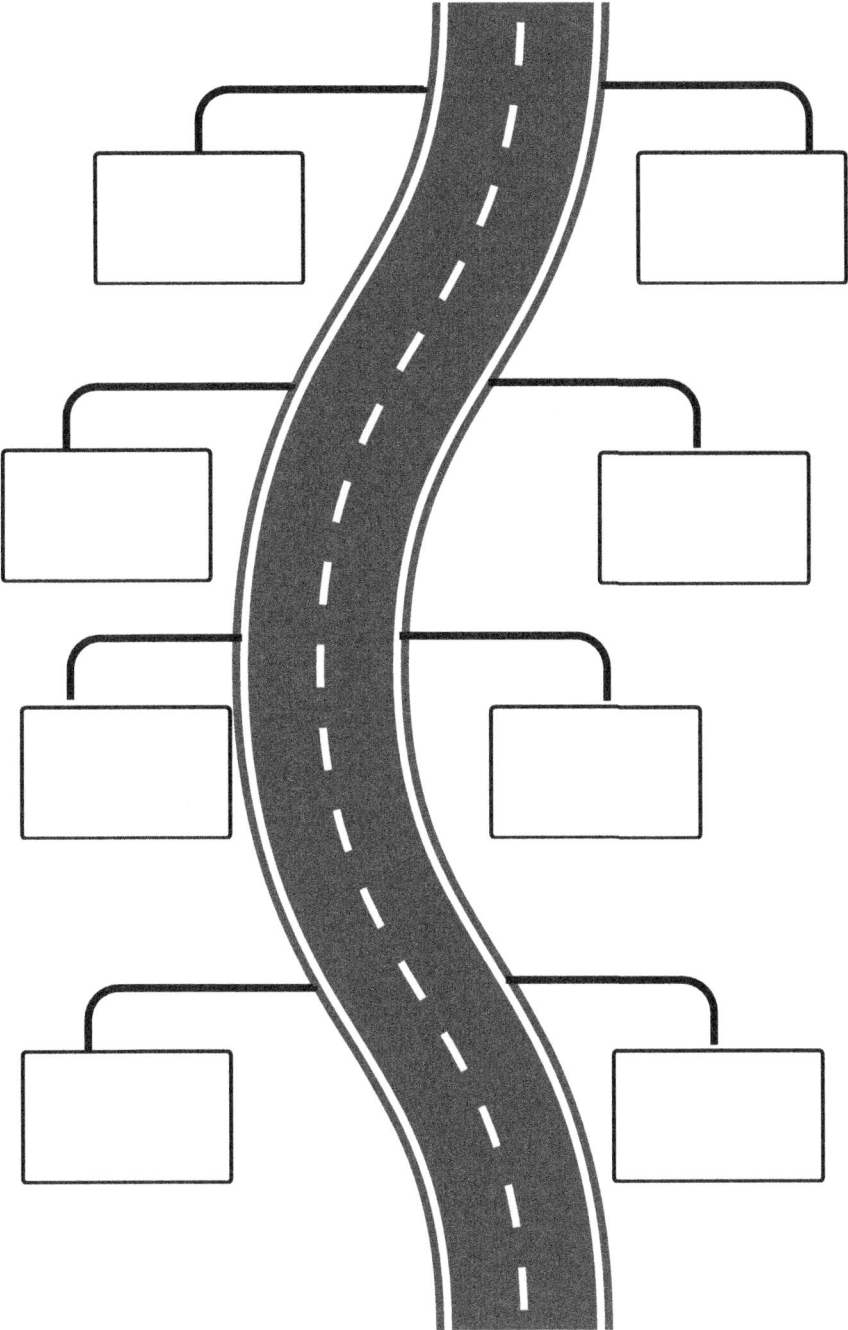

Memory Lane

Memories

My Ticket

My Experience

....
....
....
....
....

My Rating

My Notes

....
....
....
....

Travel Guide

From ....

Were to go

....
....
....
....
....
....

Add map

Hotspot   Restaurant   Accomodations

Top deal

....
....
....
....
....

Attraction

....
....
....
....
....

Local Friend

Remember the people you have met

Draw them

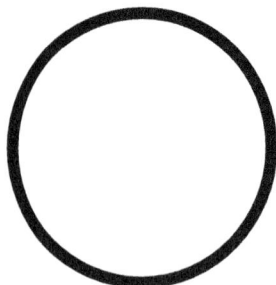

Memories

Memories

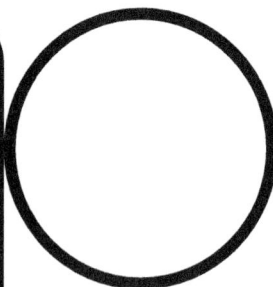

Keep in touch

Name _____

Phone _____

Address _____

Email _____

Travel Album

Stick your photo here

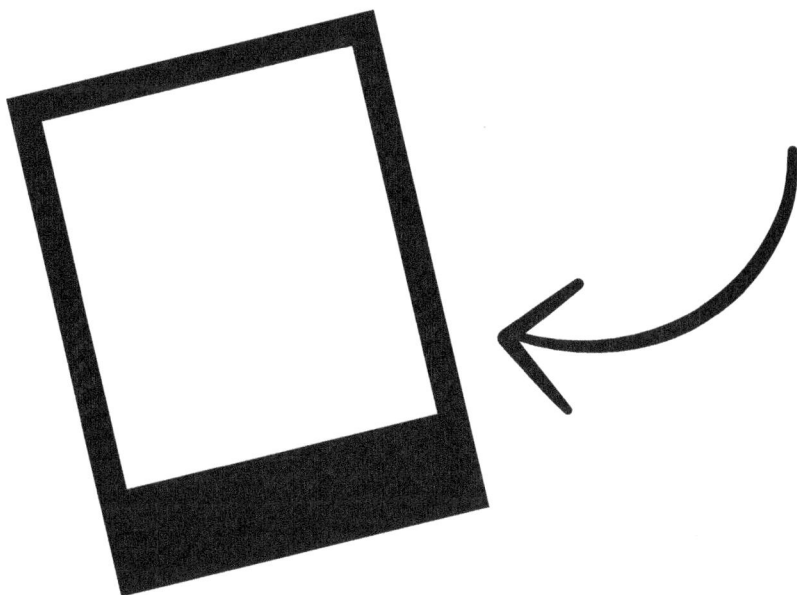

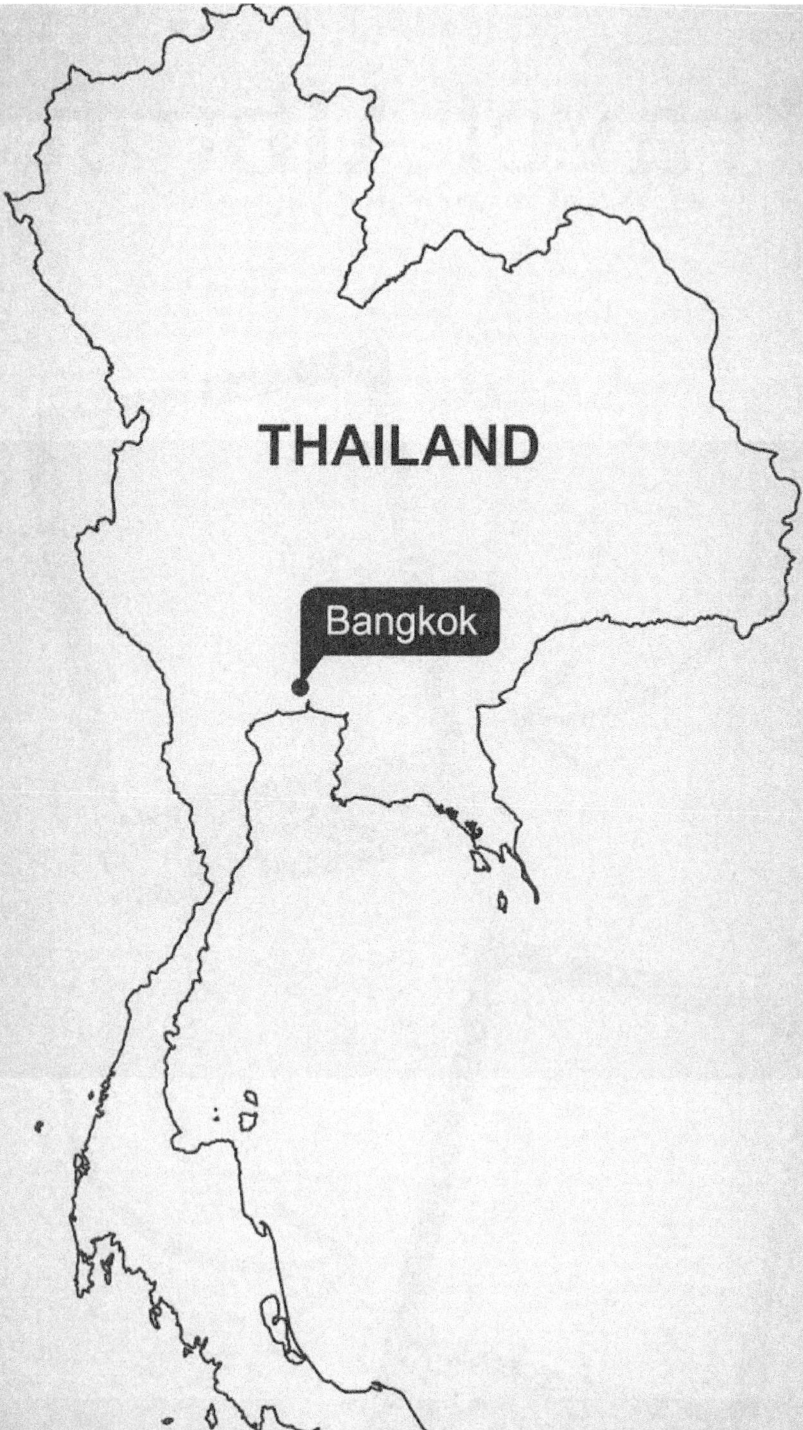
THAILAND
Bangkok

A Moment

"Dear readers, your thoughts are cherished! If this literary voyage has left you with insights, laughter, or a newfound perspective, I kindly request you to take a moment and drop a review. Your feedback is invaluable, and every word contributes to refining future chapters. Let your voice be the compass guiding this narrative journey. Thank you for sharing your thoughts – corrections, compliments, or quirks, they're all welcome aboard!"

Printed in Great Britain
by Amazon